The Best of Two Kitchens

Susan Kyllonen & Myrtle Royse

Balboa Press books may be ordered through booksellers or by contacting:

Balboa Press
A Division of Hay House
1663 Liberty Drive
Bloomington, IN 47403
www.balboapress.com
1 (877) 407-4847

ISBN: 978-1-9822-2816-3 (sc)
ISBN: 978-1-9822-2817-0 (e)

Library of Congress Control Number: 2019906906

Print information available on the last page.

Balboa Press rev. date: 06/15/2019

BALBOA
PRESS
A DIVISION OF HAY HOUSE

Acknowledgement

We want to sincerely thank everyone who is excited about our new Cookbook "The Best of Two Kitchens". We were fortunate to have the location of the VFW in Bellevue, WA with a supportive work staff & high-speed internet. Marla was very attentive to both Myrtle & me while we were busy writing & creating.

My beautiful daughter Chevonne was essential in the creation of the front & back covers. She has a very fun & colorful side that was so necessary for our artist to create the covers.

Chevonne's friend Tanya, jumped in when the publisher needed a different format. A different format? Myrtle & I didn't really know what that was. For that, we thank her for all her techie expertise.

Jamie Jo, my beautiful girlfriend, saved the day for us. She has the Apple laptop knowledge and the savvy to help us get this book to the publisher.

God Bless Everyone!

Our Advice

All of the information in this cookbook, we picked up along the way by talking to friends face to face or over the telephone. Other information we got from reading books & magazines or listening to the radio. Advice does not constitute medical & should not be misconstrued as such.

We do not guarantee the safety or effectiveness of any drug, treatment or advice mentioned. Some of our tips may not be effective for everyone.

All that we can say is that we have tested & tried many of these ideas & it has kept us above ground for a total of 164 years. So do what you want, try our ideas & suggestions at your own risk. Just remember, that a good Doctor is the best judge of what medical treatment you may need.

Please try our recipes
They are all brand new
We enjoyed making them
And hope that you will too

We use ingredients that
Will make you strong
Stick to the directions &
You won't go wrong

If you want to make changes
Well that would be nice
But choose healthy ingredients
That's Our Advice

Keep a Smile on your Face

When you walk into your kitchen

With a smile upon your face

You must always be greeted

By fresh flowers in a lovely vase.

Keep your kitchen charming

Kitchens should be charming

And a place you'll love to be

Enjoying a cup of coffee

Or sipping on some tea.

Special Prayer

Let us give thanks for all the good things in life. Help all of us to have better health.

Help those who are ill & give them comfort. Strengthen all of us to enjoy each day. Help us all to get across all obstacles that we might be confronted with. Bless our lives & this food with your great healing power.

Amen

Contents

Cocktail Order

Myrtle's Martini *

Rum Swizzle

Susan's
Manhattan *

Vodka Jubilee

Gin Zinger

Salty Dawg *

Whiskey Standard *

Myrtle's Margarita *

Vodka Twister

GrassHopper *

Apple Jack Cooler

Grapefruit Vodka
Delight

Susan's Famous
Bloody Mary

Sweet Patoote

Tangle Foot

Myrtle's Martini

1 jigger Gin

1/4 jigger Dry Vermouth

1/4 jigger Sweet Italian Vermouth

Garnish with 2 Stuffed Green Olives

Shake 46 times (Myrtle's Secret) with Ice & Strain.

Rum Swizzle

2 jiggers of Jamaican Rum

1/2 Lime (fresh & squeezed)

1 tsp Organic Sugar

Dash of Bitters

Dash of Pernod

Stir until chilled. Pour into a tall glass filled with shaved Ice. Mix well with Swizzle Stick.

Susan's Manhattan

1 1/2 jiggers of Crown Royal

1/3 jigger of Sweet Vermouth

1 dash Bitters

Stir with Ice & Strain. Serve with a Cherry.

Vodka Jubilee

1 1/2 jigger of Absolute Vodka

1 jigger of Cherry Brandy

1 jigger of Orange Juice

Stir well with Ice. Strain into a cocktail glass.

Gin Zinger

1 jigger of Tangueray Gin

1/4 jigger Lime Juice (freshly squeezed)

1 tsp Organic Sugar

6 dashes Bitters

Pour ingredients into pitcher & add shaved Ice.

Mix until the pitcher begins to frost.

Strain into cocktail glass & serve.

Salty Dawg

2 jiggers Tangueray Gin

4 jiggers Grapefruit Juice (freshly squeezed)

Fill a tall glass with shaved Ice & pour in Gin & Grapefruit

Juice. Add a pinch of Himalayan Salt. Stir well.

Whiskey Standard

2 jiggers Crown Royal

1/2 tsp of Organic Sugar

1 dash Bitters

Put sugar in Old Fashioned Glass, then add Ice, Bitters & Whiskey. Garnish with Cherry, Orange Slice & a Lemon Twist.

Myrtle's Margarita

1 1/2 jigger Tequila

1/2 jigger of Triple Sec

1/2 jigger Lime Juice (freshly sqeezed)

Shake with Ice & Strain into a chilled cocktail glass frosted with Salt. A slice of Lime on edge of glass.

Vodka Twister

1 jigger of Absolute Vodka

1/2 tbl Lime Juice (freshly squeezed) Lemon Soda

Serve in highball glass with Ice. Add a Lime peel.

Grasshopper

1/2 jigger White Breme de Cacao

1/2 jigger Green Creme de Menthe

1/2 jigger of Heavy Cream

Shake with cracked Ice.

Strain into a cocktail glass & Garnish with one sprig of a Mint Leaf

Apple Jack Cooler

2 jiggers Applejack

1/2 tbl Lemon (freshly squeezed)

1 tbl Organic Sugar

Shake with Ice & Strain into cocktail glass.

Add a couple cubes of Ice & fill the rest with Soda Water.

Grapefruit Delight

1 lg Ruby Grapefruit

1 1/2 jiggers of Potato Vodka

1/2 Lemon (freshly squeezed) Himalayan Salt around Rim Ice Cubes

Squeeze Grapefruit in a glass, add Vodka, & squeeze 1/2 Lemon. Mix.

Susan's Special Bloody Mary

2 jiggers of Potato Vodka

1 tbl Olive Juice

1/2 tsp Horseradish

Himalayan Salt & Fresh Ground Pepper

1/2 Lime (freshly squeezed)

1/2 tbl Worcestershire Sauce

Bloody Mary Mix

Tabasco Sauce

Add Olives, Pepper Jack Cheese, Shrimp, Bacon, Celery Stalk, pickled bean, pickled Asparagus.

Sweet Patootie

1 1/2 jigger Dry Gin

1/2 jigger Cointreau

1/2 jigger Orange Juice

Stir with Ice & Strain into glass.

TangleFoot

2 jiggers Light Rum

1 jigger Orange Juice

1/2 jigger Lemon Juice (freshly sqeezed)

Shake with Ice & Strain into glass.

Hors d'oeuvres

Favorite Artichoke
& Spinach Dip

Very Veggie Dip

Hot Crab Dip

Avocado Party Dip

Super Salmon Roll

Spinach Dip

Susan's Bruschetta

Tapenade Cracker
Bites

Crab & Avocado
Crisps

Warm Olives w
Garlic, Lemon &
Rosemary

Prosciutto w Grilled
Squash Ribbons w
Mint Dressing

Stilton w Fig
Pastries

Caper Cream
Cheese w Smoked
Fish

Peanut Chicken w
Chili Mayo

Mango Shrimp w
Endive

Favorite Artichoke & Spinach Dip

1/2 cup Parmesan Cheese (grated)

1/4 cup Romano Cheese (grated)

2 Garlic cloves

1/2 tsp Garlic Salt

1/2 tsp Basil

1 Artichokes (14 oz can)

1/2 Spinach (frozen, thawed & drained)

Mix in blender. When pureed, place in baking dish & bake at 400 degrees un- til brown on the top.

Serve hot with delicious Crackers of your choice or Baguette rounds…

Very Vegetable Dip

Combine in blender:

1 cup Mayonnaise

2 cups Cottage Cheese

3/4 cup chopped Green Onions

1 1/2 tsp prepared Horseradish

1 1/2 tsp Worcestershire Sauce

1 1/2 tsp Caraway seeds

1 1/2 tsp Celery seeds

1 tsp Garlic Salt

4 shakes Tabasco

Blend until well mixed. Garnish top with chopped Green Onions. Serve chilled with a tray of assorted raw vegetables.

Hot Crab Dip

In a bowl, cream together…

7 oz Crab Meat

8 oz whipped Cream Cheese (softened)

1 tsp non fat Milk

1 tsp Lemon (freshly squeezed)

2 tsp Curry Powder

Salt & Pepper to taste

Crackers (any kind you prefer)

Stir in a 7 oz can of drained Crab Meat.

Bake in a heatproof crock-pot at 350 degrees for 20 - 25 minutes. Serve hot with Crackers. Makes 1 1/2 cups.

Avocado Party Dip

3 Avocados (ripe, peeled, seeded and coarsely mashed)

1 tsp Himalayan Salt

1 tbl Lemon or Lime (freshly squeezed)

1/8 tsp Worcestershire Sauce

1 clove Garlic (crushed)

2 med Tomatoes (peeled, seeded and finely chopped)

Combine all ingredients. Cover & chill.

Makes approx. 4 cups of Avocado "Guacamole" Dip.

Serve with crunchy Tortilla or Corn Chips.

Super Salmon Roll

1 can Salmon (drained)

1 8 oz pkg Cream Cheese

1/4 - 3/4 tsp Horseradish

1 tsp Lemon (freshy squeezed)

1/4 tsp Himalayan Salt

1 Garlic clove (minced)

2 tsp Purple Onion (chopped)

Mix all ingredients together & let set until firm in refrigerator. Roll into a ball & keep rolling in Parsley Flakes & chopped Walnuts. Optional: Tiny bit of liquid smoke.

Special Spinach Dip

1 cup Best Foods Mayonnaise

1 1/2 cups Sour Cream

1 1/2 10 oz pkg of frozen chopped Spinach

1 pkg Knorr Vegetable Soup

1 8 oz can Water Chestnuts (sliced)

3 Green Onions (sliced)

Mix all together & put in a bowl or a hollowed out loaf of round bread. Cut top lid & hollow out part into squares to serve with it.

Susan's Bruschetta

1 1/2 lbs Cherry Tomatoes (quartered)

3 cloves of Garlic (minced)

1 1/4 tsp Extra Virgin Olive Oil

1 1/4 tsp Balsamic Vinegar

7 Basil Leaves (fresh and chopped)

3/4 tsp Himalayan Salt

3/4 tsp Ground Pepper (fresh)

1 Baguette of Italian Bread

1/4 cup Extra Virgin Olive Oil

Take the top seven ingredients & mix in a bowl.

Half the Baguette long ways & pour the Organic Olive Oil down the middle on both halves.

Brown in a pan, then put the Bruschetta mixture all over the browned top.

Tapenade Cracker Bites

1 1/2 cups pitted Kalamata Olives

2 Anchovy Filets (minced)

3 1/4 tbl Capers (rinsed)

2 tbl Parsley (fresh & chopped)

3 cloves of Garlic (roasted)

3 1/2 tbl Lemon Juice (freshly sqeezed)

Salt & Pepper to taste

1/3 cup Extra Virgin Olive Oil

1 tbl Brandy

Mix all together & put on Crackers or Crustini's.

Crab & Avocado Crisps

2/3 cup Jicama (finely grated)

1 Avocado (finely diced)

1/2 Lime Zest (finely grated)

1/2 Lime Juice (fresh)

1 1/2 Celery (stalk finely diced)

2 Green Onions (thinly sliced)

2 tsp Cilantro (finely chopped)

1/2 cup Crabmeat (fresh)

2 1/2 cups Mayonnaise

Head of Romaine

Baguette Crisps

Toss gently all ingredients together & chill for a couple of hours in fridge.

Serve on a bed of Romaine Lettuce (chopped) with Baguette Crisps.

Warm Olives with Herbs & Garlic

1/4 Cup Extra Virgin Olive Oil

1 Lemon (strips of Zest)

1 Rosemary Sprig

2 1/2 cloves of Garlic (thickly sliced)

3 cups using 1 cup Kalamata, 1 cup Nicoise & 1 cup green Sicilian Olives

In a saucepan, combine the Oil with the Lemons Zest, Rosemary & Garlic. Moderate heat until the Garlic browns (about 5 min).

Remove from heat & stir in the Olives & marinate for 15 min. A nice side dish.

Proscuitto w Squash Ribbons

1 1/2 tsp Lime Zest (finely grated)

1/4 Lime Juice (fresh)

1/3 cup Mint (chopped)

2 Garlic Cloves (finely chopped)

1/3 cup Extra Virgin Olive Oil (you may need more)

Salt & Pepper to taste

2 medium Zucchini (very thinly sliced lengthwize)

2 medium Yellow Squash (very thinly sliced lengthwize)

6 oz Prosciutto (thinly sliced)

Preheat BBQ. While BBQ is heating, combine the Lime Zest, Juice with Mint, 1/3 cup Olive Oil, Salt & Pepper. On 12 inch Skewers, add a chunk of Zucchini, chunk of Yellow Squash, a slice of Prosciutto and alternate. Brush the Olive Oil on Zucchini, Yellow Squash & Prosciutto. Salt & Pepper to taste. Grill the skewers over high heat

Stilton w Fig Pastries

Puff Pastry (320 g pack)

2 1/4 tbl Whole Milk

1/3 lb Stilton

3 Figs (large)

1/4 cup Walnuts

1/2 cup Arugula

Preheat oven to 400 degrees. Roll out the Puff Pastry into a rectangle on a floured surface. Put on a baking tray. Score the edges of rectangle so when baking, the edges will puff up. Brush the edge with a little Milk.

Divide the Stilton into tiny chunks or use a grater & evenly spread half over Pastry. Slice the Figs into rounds & evenly place on Puff Pastry. Add Crumbled Walnuts. Add a little more Stilton.

Bake for 10 min, add a little more Milk on Crust, reduce oven to 375 F degrees & bake 15 more min. Let cool for 10 min & add the other half of Stilton & sprinkle the Arugula over the top.

Caper Cream Cheese w Smoked Salmon

6 oz Smoked Salmon (shredded)

4 oz Sour Cream

8 oz Cream Cheese (room temperature)

4 dashes Worcestershire Sauce

1/4 cup Capers (drained)

In medium bowl, beat Sour Cream & Cream Cheese. Add shredded Smoke

Salmon, Worcestershire & Capers.

Refrigerate for three hours & serve with your favorite Crackers.

Peanut Chicken w Chili Mayo

1/2 cup Panko Bread Crumbs

3/4 cup Peanuts (roasted w salt) (finely chopped)

1/3 cup Cilantro (fresh & chopped)

Himalayan Salt & fresh Ground Pepper

2 Chicken Breasts (skinless, cut into thin strips)

3 tbs Extra Virgin Olive Oil

1/2 cup Mayonnaise

2 tsp Asian Chili Garlic Sauce

On a large platter, mix the Peanuts, Panko, Cilantro & 1/2 tsp Salt & 1/2 tsp Pepper. Thread each Chicken Strip on a 12 inch skewer & coat w Peanut mixture. Try & press the Peanut mixture into the Chicken. Then heat up a large skillet with the Olive Oil & cook the Chicken 2 min on each side. Serve with the mixed Mayonnaise w Asian Chili Garlic Sauce.

Mango Shrimp w Endive

1/2 Mango (finely sliced) (1 cup)

1/2 lb Shrimp (cooked, peeled & chopped)

2 tbl Extra Virgin Olive oil

Himalayan Salt & Fresh Ground Pepper

2 tbl Cilantro (fresh & chopped)

1 tbl Lime Juice (freshly squeezed)

2 tsp Ginger (fresh & grated)

Endive Leaves

In a medium bowl, blend the Mango, Shrimp, Cilantro, Lime Juice, Oil, Ginger, 1/4 tsp Salt & 1/8 tsp Pepper. Spoon this mixture into the Endive Leaves.

Before Soups & Salads

Hi! Here we are again. We hope that you didn't stuff yourself with the appetizers. So that you won't have room left in your stomach for the soups & salads that we are going to present to you. One thing for sure, all of these recipes are very tasty, yet full of all healthful ingredients.

Soups & Chowders

Hearty Beef

Borscht (Tasty Soup)

Myrtle's Hearty Potato Soup

Marvelous Minestrone Soup

Stunning Spinach Soup

Mediterranean Chicken Lemon Soup

Hearty Ham & Pea Soup

Sassy Salmon Chowder

Wild Mushroom Creamy Soup

Frenchy Onion Soup

Crazy Good Carrot Soup

Deelish Chicken Chili

Broccoli-Cheddar Soup

Corn Chowder

South Western Corn & Chicken Soup

Hearty Beef Stew

1 lb Prime Beef (chopped)

1 1/4 cups Onion (chopped)

3 1/2 cups Water

1 1/2 cups Celery (finely chopped)

1 cup Carrots (chopped)

1 cup Potatoes (diced)

1 28 oz can Tomatoes

2 Bay Leaves

2 tbs Worcestershire Sauce

2 tsp Himalayan Salt

1/4 tbs Pepper (fresh ground)

Using a large saucepan, cook Beef until brown.

Drain off fat. Then add Onions & stir in the rest of the ingredients. Heat to boiling, reduce heat & simmer until vegetables are tender. Serves 6.

Borscht (Tasty Soup)

4 1/2 cups Beets (coarsely shredded)

1 1/2 cups Onion (chopped)

7 cups of Beef Broth

1 tbs Beef Bouillon Granules

2 1/4 cups Cabbage (thinly sliced)

2 1/4 cups Carrots (chopped in 1/2 inch chunks)

1 1/4 Celery (thinly sliced)

3 tbs Brown Sugar

1/2 tsp Black Pepper

1/4 cup White Vinegar

Topping: 1 1/2 cups of nonfat Sour Cream plus 3 tbs Dill (fresh & minced)

Combine the Beets, Carrots, Onion, Celery, Broth, Brown Sugar, Bouillon & Pepper in a 4 qt pot & bring to a boil.

Reduce heat to low, cover & simmer for 20 minutes or until vegetables are tender. Add Cabbage, simmer uncovered for 15 minutes or until Cabbage is done. Remove pot from heat & stir in Vinegar.

Top each serving with a rounded tablespoon of Sour Cream & sprinkling of Dill. Yum!!!

Myrtle's Hearty Potato Soup

6 medium Yukon Potato's (peeled & cubed)

2 Carrots (cubed)

6 Celery Stalk (diced)

2 quarts Water

1 White Onion chopped

6 tbl Butter

6 tsp Whole Wheat Flour

1 tsp Himalayan Salt

1/2 tsp Pepper

1 1/2 cup non fat Milk

Cook vegetables & water until tender (about 20 minutes). Drain reserving liquid & set vegetables aside. In same kettle, saute Onion in Butter until soft. Stir in Flour, Salt & Pepper. Gradually add Milk stirring until thickened. Gently stir in cooled vegetables… now add 1 cup or more of reserved liquid until soup is of desired consistency…. 8 to 10 servings

Marvelous Minestrone Soup

13 oz can crushed Tomatoes

5 slices of thin Bacon (chopped)

3 tbl Extra Virgin Olive Oil

14 oz can Cannellini Beans, drain & rinse

4 tbls of fresh Parsley (chopped)

Salt & Pepper

3 Carrots (chopped)

3 Celery Stalks (finely chopped)

1 qt Chicken Stock

1/4 cup of Brown Rice

Parmesan (shaved)

In large saucepan, gently heat Olive Oil & cook Bacon for three minutes before adding Carrots, Celery, & Onion. Cook until soft. Then add the Tomatoes & Garlic. Add Stock. Add Salt & Pepper to taste. Bring to boil. Now simmer for 10 minutes. Add Rice & simmer another 15 minutes. Now add the Beans. Put the lid on & simmer for 20 more minutes. Can add extra Stock if necessary. Stir in half of the Parsley. Serve in warm bowl adding the Parmesan Cheese & rest of Parsley on top.

Stunning Spinach Soup

1/4 cup White Onion (chopped)

1/2 large clove Garlic (minced)

1 tbl Butter

1 lg can Chicken Broth (46 oz)

1 cup Orzo Pasta (uncooked)

1/4 tsp Nutmeg

1/8 tsp Pepper

1 pkg (10 oz) Frozen Spinach

Cook Onion & Garlic in Butter in large pot till soft.

Add Chicken Broth & bring to a boil.

Add Pasta, Nutmeg & Pepper.

Simmer for 5 minutes.

Add Spinach. Bring to boil & simmer for 5 minutes, stirring often. Season with more Pepper & sprinkle Parmesan Cheese on the top! Yum!!!

Mediterranean Chicken Lemon Soup

2 (14 oz) Chicken Broth

1/2 cup Brown Rice

2 cups Carrots (sliced 1/2 in chunks)

2 cups Chicken (chopped)

1/2 cup Red Pepper strips

1/4 cup Lemon (freshly squeezed)

1 clove Garlic (chopped)

12 oz can fat free Milk

1 tsp Cornstarch

3/4 to 1 cup Basil (chopped)

Bring broth to boil. Add Rice & Carrots, simmer until Carrots are tender. Stir in Chicken, Bell Pepper, Lemon & Garlic. Cook 5 minutes more. Combine Milk & bring to just a boil. Remove from heat, season with Salt & Pepper. Garnish with chopped Basil.

Hearty Ham & Pea Soup

3 1/4 cups of dried Green Split Peas, (soaked overnight in water & drained)

1 Ham Bone wih lots of meat (1 lb)

1 qt of Water

1/1/2 qts Chicken Stock

3 Potatoes (diced)

4 Celery Stalks, (slice fine)

3 Leeks (sliced)

1 1/2 White Onions (minced) Salt & Pepper

1 tsp Caraway Seeds

1 tsp Thyme (fresh & chopped)

3/4 tsp Nutmeg

1 tbl Lemon Juice (freshly squeezed) Sprigs of Thyme to decorate

In a large saucepan, add Ham Bone, Water & Stock. Bring to a boil, then turn the heat down to simmer & cover for an hour. Add Split Peas & cook for another hour. Now add Potatoes, Celery, Leeks & Spices. Cook for 30 minutes. Now remove the Ham Bone, cut away all the meat, shred it& put the meat aside. In a food processor, take 1/2 the soup & blend until smooth. Return to pan & add the blended soup. Mix together & serve hot. Decorate with Thyme.

Sassy Salmon Chowder

1 can Salmon

1 clove Garlic (minced)

1/2 ea cup Onion, Celery & Green Pepper

3 tsp Butter

1 cup each Carrots & Potatoes

2 cups Chicken Broth

1 tsp Himalayan Salt

1/2 tsp Pepper (freshly ground)

1/2 tsp Thyme

1/2 cup Frozen Peas

1 Can Creamed Corn

1 (13 oz) can evaporated Milk

1 tbl Parsley (fresh)

Sauté Garlic, Celery, Green Pepper in Butter. Add Chicken Broth, Potatoes & Carrots w seasonings. Cover & simmer for 20 minutes. Add Peas & cook for 5 min. Add Salmon, Corn & Milk. Heat through. Do not BOIL. Sprinkle top with Parsley.

Wild Mushroom Creamy Soup

1 1/2 cups of Morels, Shitake Mushrooms

3 Garlic cloves (minced)

1 qt Chicken Stock

1 1/2 cup of reduced fat Sour Cream

1 Onion (chopped)

1 tbl Extra Virgin Olive Oil

1 large Gold Potato, (finely diced)

Chop Mushrooms finely, leaving a few whole ones for the garnish. Cook the Onion & Potato with 1 tsp Olive Oil for about 10 minutes. Then put in a blender with 1/2 of the Chicken Stock & blend until smooth. In a saucepan, put the Mushrooms, Garlic with 2 tsp of Olive Oil & sauté for about 5 minutes. Take out the whole Mushrooms & save for garnish. Combine Potato mixture with the Sour Cream in a large bowl. Add a big spoon of hot Stock to Cream mixture stirring. Stir in another couple of big spoons of hot Stock. Now add everything to the pan & mix. Reheat. Season with Salt & Pepper.

Serve in warm bowls with the whole Mushrooms on top. Serves 4.

Frenchy Onion Soup

1 3/4 lb Onions (about 6 large onions) (thinly sliced)

6 cups Beef Stock

4 1/2 tbls Extra Virgin Olive Oil

3 cloves of Garlic (minced)

3 tbls Apple Juice

1 1/2 cups White Wine (Dry) Salt & Pepper Croutons:

10 oz Guyere Cheese 10

1 1/4 Extra Virgin Olive Oil

2 Garlic cloves (minced)

4 slices Rye Bread, cut in half

Chives

In a heavy saucepan, heat the Olive Oil, adding Apple Juice, Onions, & Garlic, high heat, stirring constantly for about 5 minutes. Turn down heat to simmer for about 20 minutes. The color of the bottom of pan should turn a caramel brown. Now pour the Stock & Wine into Onion Mix with Salt & Pepper to taste.

Using a wooden spoon, stir scraping all the juice from the sides & the bottom of pan. Simmer for about an hour (uncovered pan).

While the Onion Mixture is simmering, make the Croutons by putting Olive Oil on a cookie sheet, adding the Garlic. Place the Rye bread in the oil, turning to make sure both sides are coated. Preheat oven to 350 degrees. Bake for about 15 minutes until crunchy & crispy. Now spread the Guyere Cheese thickly on the croutons. Heat the broiler on high. Pour soup in heatproof bowls, add the two halves of Croutons in each bowl. Put in broiler until the cheese bubbles. Place the Chives over the soup with Croutons for garnish and serve.

Crazy Good Carrot Soup

3 1/2 Carrots (chopped)

1 White Onion (chopped)

1 tbl Extra Virgin Olive Oil

2 Bayleaves

Cilantro (a small bunch, leaves separated from stems)

1 1/4 qts Vegetable Stock

Salt & Pepper

4 tbl Greek Plain Yogurt

Heat Olive Oil in a saucepan. Add Onion, Garlic & Bay Leaves in pan. Add Cilantro stems, Stock & bring to boil. After you cool the soup, put in food processor without the Bay Leaves & blend until smooth. Gently reheat. Season with Salt & Pepper. Finely chop 1/2 of the Cilantro leaves & stir into soup. Serve the soup in warm bowls, add a tbl of Yogurt with the remaining Cilantro leaves. Serves 4.

Deelish Chicken Chili

1 can Hominy (25 oz) (rinsed & drained)

3 cans Cannellini Beans (15 oz) (rinsed & drained)

2 1/2 cups Butternut Squash (cubed)

2 tbl Cumin

2 Oregano Sprigs

1 1/2 lb Boneless Chicken Thighs

6 tbl fresh Cilantro (cut up)

3 oz Cheddar Cheese (shredded)

1 Jalapeno (thinly sliced) Lime Wedges

3 1/2 Chicken Stock

1 cup Onion (chopped)

1 1/4 tbl Chili Powder

3/4 Himalayan Salt

3 Garlic Cloves (minced)

1 can Green Chiles (5 oz) (diced & drained)

1/3 cup Plain Yogurt

1/3 cup Green Onions (chopped)

In a food processor, puree 1 can of Beans. Place puree, w cans of Beans, Hominy, & the next ingredients, reserving 1 tbl Green Chilies in a Slow Cooker (6 qt). Add a tbl Green Chilies & the Chicken Thighs. Cook on Low for 8 hours. Take Thighs out & shred. Stir shredded Thighs back in Slow Cooker. Keep warm. Process reserved 1 tbl Green Chilies, 2 tbl Cilantro & Yogurt in a Cuisinart Processor. Place the Chili in separate bowls…. Top with the Yogurt, Cliantro, Cheese, Jalapeno & Green Onions. Serve with Lime Wedges.

Broccoli-Cheddar Soup

1 White Onion (chopped)

1 (14 1/2 oz) Organic Chicken Broth

1 1/2 cups Cheddar Cheese (shredded)

Pinch of Himalayan Salt

2 cups Broccoli Florets

1 tsp Extra Virgin Olive Oil

2 cups Non Fat Milk

1/2 cup Wheat Flour

Pinch of Pepper (freshly ground)

In large saucepan, sauté Onion in Olive Oil for 10 minutes. Stir in Flour, Salt & Pepper. Cook stirring for 2 minutes. Add Broth, Milk, Broccoli. Bring to boil & cover. Cook on low for 10 minutes. Puree soup in batches. Bring to boil in saucepan. Remove from heat & stir in cheese…. Serves 4. YUM!!!

Corn Chowder

1 small Onion (diced)

3 ears Corn (cut off cob)

Pinch of Salt & Pepper

1 1/2 cups Cauliflower Florets

2 1/2 cup Skim Milk

1 (7 oz) Plain Greek Yogurt

1/2 bunch of Green Onions (thinly sliced)

Heat Dutch oven…. Spray Pam…. Medium hot…. Add Onion & Corn. Season with Salt & Pepper. Sauté 6 minutes till vegetables start to soften. Add Cauliflower & Milk, cover& bring to a boil… simmer for 20 minutes until vegetables are tender. Strain 1-cup liquid… return to pot. Pour rest of liquid with vegetables & blend until smooth. Now mix all the soup & bring to boil. Remove from heat & stir in Yogurt and Scallions. Season with herbs & serve. Serves 4

South Western Corn & Chicken Soup

1 White Onion (chopped)

1/2 tsp Chili Powder

3/4 tsp Cumin

1 can Organic Chicken Broth

1 can Chopped Tomatoes

1 (10 oz) Corn Kernels (frozen)

1 (12 oz) evaporate Skim Milk

2 cups cooked Chicken (in bite size pieces)

Spray large Saucepan with Pam & place over medium heat. Cook Onions for 10 minutes until soft. Add Chili Powder & Cumin. Stir well. Add Tomatoes & Frozen Corn. Cook 4-5 minutes. Slowly pour in Milk & heat. Do not BOIL! Add Chicken, heat & mix well.

Salads

Beet Chicory Salad
w Pine Nuts

Perfect Pear

Strawberry Chicken
Pecan

Dinner Coleslaw

Arugula Chicken
Pasta

Carrot w Pistachios

Tomato, Bacon,
Greens Pasta

Cranberry Broccoli
Almond

Egg, Bacon & Kale

Mango Shrimp w
Super Greens

Pomegranate
Breakfast

Cherry Lentil &
Barley

Myrtle's Ceasar
Canlis

Pineapple Surprise

Avocado Citrus
w Creamy Poppy
Dressing

Beets, Chicory Salad w Pine Nut Dressing

1 Belgium Endive, (halved lengthwise, cored & torn into bite size pieces)

1 head of Escarole (white & light leaves only) torn

3/4 head of Radicchio, (cored & torn into bite size pieces)

3 tbl Pine Nuts

3 1/2 tbl Extra Virgin Olive Oil

3 1/2 tbl Sherry Vinegar

2 cloves of Garlic (minced)

1 1/2 tsp Organic Honey

Salt & Pepper

3 Beets (scrubbed & sliced very thin)

1 med Fennel Bulb (halved lengthwise, cored and very thinly slices)

Put the Escarole, Radicchio & Endive in an ice bath for 25 min. Meanwhile, in a small frying pan, toast the Pine Nuts until golden & fragrant (about 5 min) Let cool, transfer to a food processor & add Oil, Vinegar, Garlic, Honey & season with Salt & Pepper. Puree until smooth.

Drain the greens & spin dry. Using a chilled bowl, add the Beets & sliced Fennel. Toss well.

Drizzle 1/2 the dressing around bowl & season with Salt & Pepper. Drizzle the remaining dressing & toss again. Top with Fennel Fronds & serve right away.

Pear Salad

2 cups Pears (diced)

1 1/4 cups Celery (chopped)

1/3 cup Pecans (chopped)

Bunch of Red Grapes Lettuce Leaves

.

Dressing: Mix 2 tbls Flour, 1/4 tsp Stevia, 2 tbls fresh Lemon Juice together. Cook over low heat until flour is cooked & clear. Cool.

Mix the Celery & Pears in the dressing, add Nuts. Serve on Lettuce Leaves. Garnish with Grapes.

Strawberry Chicken Pecan Salad

4 tsp Extra Virgin Olive Oil

2 tsp Honey

1/2 tsp Black Pepper (freshly ground)

2 1/2 cups halved Strawberries

1/4 tsp Paprika

4 cups Baby Spinach

5 tbl Toasted Pecans (crumbled)

1 tbl White Balsamic Vinegar

3/4 tsp Thyme (chopped)

1/4 tsp Himalayan Salt

2 1/4 cups Boneless Chicken Breast

Cooking Spray

1/2 cup Red Onion (thinly sliced)

1/3 cup Feta Cheese (crumbled)

Combine 1 tbl Oil, Vinegar, Honey, Thyme, 1/4 Pepper & 1/2 tsp Salt in a bowl and whisk. Add 1 cup Strawberries tossing to coat. Let stand 10 min.

Heat up a med skillet over med-high heat. Brush Chicken with remaining 1 tsp Oil. Sprinkle evenly with remaining 1/8 tsp Pepper, Salt & Paprika. Coat Pan with cooking spray & add Chicken to pan. 2 to 3 min per each side until done. Let stand 5 min & cut across the grain into slices. Divide Spinach, 1 cup Strawberries & Onion between 2 plates or shallow bowls. Evenly top with Chicken & Strawberry Balsamic mixture. Add 11/2 cups Pecans & Fetal Cheese. Yum !!!!

Dinner Coleslaw

4 cups Green Cabbage (shredded)

1 1/2 cups Shallots (thinly sliced)

1/4 cup White Vinegar

1/2 cup Extra Virgin Olive Oil

1 clove Garlic (chopped)

2 tsp Himalayan Salt

1 1/2 cups Carrots (grated)

3/4 cup Celery (thinly sliced)

2 tbl Champagne Vinegar

1 tbl Organic Sugar

1/2 cup Mayonnaise

1/2 tsp Pepper (freshly ground)

Combine Cabbage, Carrots, Shallots & Celery. Set aside. Whisk remaining ingredients.

Add dressing to vegetables. Combine & toss coating vegetables thoroughly. Put aside slaw at room temperature one hour before serving. Yum!!!

Arugula Chicken Pasta Salad

6 oz uncooked whole wheat Fusilli Pasta

2 cloves of Garlic chopped finely

2 1/2 cups of shredded boneless Chicken Breast

3/8 tsp Black Pepper

3 tsp Extra Virgin Olive Oil

1 large Tomato chopped

1 1/2 Shallot, thinly sliced

4 oz Brie Cheese (remove rind and finely chopped)

2 tsp Cider Vinegar

3/8 tsp Salt

5 1/2 oz fresh baby Arugula

Cook Pasta per directions.

Drain pasta, reserving 1/2 cooking liquid.

Place Shallot and Garlic in a small bowl.

Pour the 1/4 cup of cooking liquid. Steep for 5 min. Place Pasta and Cheese in large bowl.

Stir in Chicken, Vinegar, Shallot, Salt & 1/4 tsp Pepper.

Combine Oil and Arugula to Pasta and toss.

Sprinkle with Tomato and 1/8 tsp Pepper. Yum!!!

Carrot Salad w Pistachio's

1 (15oz) can Chickpeas

2 tbl Extra Virgin Olive Oil

1/2 tsp Himalayan Salt

1/2 tsp ground Cumin

1/4 Lemon Juice (fresh)

3 tbl Tahini

2 Garlic cloves (minced)

2 tbl Water

1/4 tsp Pepper (freshly ground)

1/4 tsp Himalayan Salt

1/4 tsp Red Pepper Flakes

5 cups Carrots (coursely chopped)

1/4 cup Fresh Parsley (coursely chopped)

3/4 shelled Pistachio's

Preheat oven to 425 degrees. Drain & rinse Chickpeas. Pat dry. Toss Chickpeas with Olive Oil, Salt & Cumin. S[read in a single layer on a baking sheet. Roast 15-20 minutes until browned & crisped, tossing occasionally. Whisk Lemon Juice, Tahini, Oil, Water, minced Garlic, Salt Pepper & Red Pepper Flakes. Combine Carrots, Parsley with all the other ingredients. Save a few Pistachio's for topping. Yum!

Tomato, Bacon, Greens Pasta Salad

2 1/2 tsp Red Wine Vinegar

1 1/4 tsp Himalayan Salt

2 tsp Dijon Mustard

2 tbl Extra Virgin Olive Oil

2 1/2 tsp Shallots (thinly sliced)

1/2 tsp Pepper (fresh ground)

3 cups baby Spinach

10 Cherry Tomotoes (cut in half)

8 oz Spiral Pasta

1/2 cup Basil Leaves (torn)

1 1/2 Avocado (peeled, pitted & cubed)

4 slices Bacon (cooked & crumbled)

In a large bowl, whisk Vinegar, Mustard, Oil, Shallots, Pepper & 1/4 tsp of Salt.

Add Spinach & Tomatoes, toss together & set aside.

Boil Pasta until al dente. Drain, while Pasta is hot add to vinaigrette bowl.

Add half of Basil & gently toss. Top with Avocado, Bacon, & remaining Basil. Yum!!!

Cranberry Broccoli Almond Salad

1/3 cup Red Onion (finely chopped)

1/2 cup Mayonnaise

4 tbl Greek Yogurt

1 tbl Organic Honey

1 tbl Apple Cider Vinegar

1/4 tsp Black Pepper (freshly ground)

1/4 tsp Himalayan Salt

5 1/2 cups Broccoli Florets (about 1 bunch)(coursely chopped)

3/4 cup Almonds (toasted & slivered)

3/4 cup Cranberries (dried)

5 Bacon slices (cooked & crumbled)

Soak Red Onion in cold water for 5 min, drain. Combine Mayonnaise, next 5 ingredients stirring with a whisk.

Stir in Red Onion, Broccoli & remaining ingredients. Cover & chill 1 1/2 hours before serving.

Egg Bacon & Kale Salad

2 large Eggs

1/2 cups Grape Tomatoes (halved)

1 1/2 tbl Extra Virgin Olive Oil

2 Bacon Slices (Cooked & Crumbled)

2 cups of Kale (Chopped)

1 1/2 tsp Apple Cider Vingear

1/8 tsp Himalayan Salt

1/8 tsp Black Pepper (Freshly Ground)

Bring a small sauce pan of water to a boil. Add both Eggs, reduce heat & simmer for 6 mins. Drain & rinse with cold water, peel eggs & set aside.

Combine Kale & Tomatoes in a bowl. Drizzle with Vinegar & Oil, sprinkle with Salt & toss. Top with Bacon finely chopped Eggs & sprinkle with more freshly ground Pepper. Yum!!!

Mango & Shrimp SuperGreen Salad

3 cups of baby Kale

2 cups of Mango (chopped)

1/2 cups Cucumber (chopped)

3 tbl Mint (fresh & chopped)

1/2 Avocado (diced)

1 lb of cooked Large Shrimp

Toss the first 5 ingredients all together. Top with the Large Shrimp. Chili Lime Dressing

Whisk together 2 1/2 tbl Lime Juice, 2 1/2 tsp Chili Powder, 1/2 tsp ground Cumin, 1/4 tsp Salt, 1 minced clove of Garlic. Whisk in 3 tbl of Extra Virgin Olive Oil.

Yum!!!

Pomegranate Breakfast Salad

4 tbl part-skim Ricotta Cheese

1 tsp Organic Honey

3/4 tsp Lemon (grated)

2 tsp Extra Virgin Olive Oil

3 cups of Spinach

1 tsp fresh Lemon or Tangerine Juice

1/3 cup Wheat Pasta

1/3 cup Pomegranate Seeds

2 tbl Roasted Almonds (coarsely chopped)

Combine first 3 ingredients in a small bowl. Combine Oil, Juice and Salt in a medium bowl. Add Spinach & Pasta. Toss everything. Arrange greens mixture in a shallow bowl & top with Pomegranate, Almonds & Ricotta mixture. Yum!!!

Cherry, Lentil & Barley Salad

Combine 1 cup of dried French Green Lentils with 1 1/4 cups of water. Bring to a boil, reduce heat, cover & simmer for 25 or minutes or until tender.

Drain & rinse, toss with 2 cups Barley & 3 pounds of fresh Cherries (pitted & halved) & 1/2 cup Feta Cheese & 1/3 cup Basil leaves (fresh & chopped)

Whisk 3 tbs of Lemon Juice, 2 tsp. Honey, 1 tsp Mustard & 3/4 tsp. Salt & a pinch of Black Pepper. Whisk in 1/4 Extra Virgin Olive Oil & add this dressing to the Barley mixture. Yum!!!

Myrtle's Ceasar Canlis

1 large head Romaine

1/2 cup chopped Green Onion

1 cup of Bacon finely chopped

1/3 tsp of Oregano

1 1/2 peeled Tomatoes

1 1/4 cup of fresh Romano Cheese

1 1/2 tbs fresh Mint finely chopped

Dressing:

1/2 cup Virgin Olive Oil

1 tsp fresh ground Pepper

1/2 tsp Himalayan Salt Croutons

1 fresh Lemon squeezed

1 coddled Egg

In large bowl, place tomatoes cut in eighths. Add sliced Romaine in bite size pieces. Add Green Onions, Cheese, Bacon, Oregano & Mint. Make the dressing, put Pepper, freshly squeezed Lemon juice with coddled Egg and whip. Slowly add Olive Oil, whipping constantly. Pour over the salad and toss. Add croutons & spread w Romano Cheese. Serves 4.

Pineapple Surprise Salad

1 pkg of Lime Jello

1 cup of Boiling Water

1 cup of Marshmallows (cut fine) Then add:

1 cup crushed Pineapple (drained)

1 cup Pineapple Juice

1 cup Walnuts (chopped)

1/2 cup Best Foods Mayonnaise

1 cup Whipped Cream

1 cup Cabbage (finely shredded)

When the jello thickens, add 1 cup Whipped Cream & 1 cup of Cabbage.

Avocado Citrus Salad

6 cups mixed Greens

2 Grapefruit (peeled & sliced horizontally)

2 Oranges (peeled & sliced horizontally)

3 ripe Avocados (seeded, peeled & sliced)

Divide the Greens on each plate. Top with plate with slices of Grapefruit, Oranges & Avocado. Drizzle the Creamy Lime Poppy dressing. Enjoy!

Creamy Lime Poppy Dressing

1/4 cup Extra Virgin Olive Oil

1/2 cup Lime Juice (freshly squeezed)

1/4 cup Organic Sugar

2 tbs Red Onion (diced)

3 tbs Mayonnaise

1 tbs White Wine Vinegar

1/4 tsp Himalayan Salt

3/4 tbs Poppy Seeds

Place all ingredients except for Poppy Seeds into a blender & blend for 30 seconds. Add the Poppy Seeds & pulse 2 times. Store in fridge in an airtight container until ready to use.

Put a song in your heart & a smile on your face. Enjoy your kitchen as a wonderful place. Choose light & vitamin filled ingredients for your entree dishes. You can change the taste & flavor a lot by using a variety of spices. Follow our recipes but feel free to make some changes to suit your own fancy.

INFORMAL
table setting

butter spreader

water glass

wine glass

bread plate

salad fork

fork

serving plate

knife

soup spoon

teaspoon

Entree's

Cacciatore with
Chicken Breasts

Beef Meatballs w
Spinach Quinoa

Glazed Salmon w
Zucchini

Chicken (Sweet &
Sour)

Cod w Green Peas

Crabby Crab
Lasagna

Turkey & Pork
Meatloaf

Scallops w Orange
& Bacon

Turkey Meatballs w
Spaghetti

Bacon Broccoli
Pizza

Pork w Pineapple

Mussels w White
Wine

Sirloin Steak w
Baked Fries

Italian Sausage
Pizza w Greens

Shrimp w Lemon
Herb Risotto

Cacciatore w Chicken Breasts

6 small boneless Chicken Breasts

10 oz. Portabello Small Mushrooms

1/4 tsp Black Pepper (freshly ground)

3 Garlic cloves (finely chopped)

1 Bay Leaf

1 cup of White Wine (dry)

1 can Tomatoes (diced)]

1/2 cup pitted Green Olives

2 1/2-tbl Extra Virgin Olive oil

1/4 tsp Himalayan Salt

1 small Onion (thinly sliced)

1 Red Bell pepper (thinly sliced)

2 tsp Fresh Rosemary (finely sliced)

8 oz. Kale (leaves chopped)

1/4 cup Fresh Parsley (chopped)

Heat oil in a deep skillet. Season Chicken w Salt & Pepper. Cook until golden brown. (3 - 4 min on each side) & then transfer to a platter. Add Mushrooms & cook until golden brown (about 4 min).

Put on platter with Chicken Breasts. Lower heat & add Red Pepper, Onion, Garlic, Rosemary & Bay Leaf & cook until tender (about 9 min). Add Wine while cooking & stirring & scraping up browned bits until reduced by half (about 3 min). Stir in Tomatoes.

Return Chicken & Mushrooms. Simmer for about 15 min with a covered pan. Fold in Kale & cook another 10 min. Take out Bay Leaf & stir in Olives & Parsley. Serve.

Beef Meatballs w Spinach & Quinoa

1 lb Ground Beef (lean)

2 tbl Extra Virgin Olive Oil

3/4 cup Quinoa (cooked)

3/4 cup Carrots (shredded)

1/2 Cup Spinach (frozen, thawed, chopped & squeezed dry)

1 Red Pepper (sliced in strips)

3 Garlic Cloves

1/2 tsp Himalayan Salt

1/2 tsp Pepper (freshly ground)

Preheat oven 400 degrees. Brush a baking pan with oil.

Combine remaining ingredients.

Shape into 16 Meatballs.

Bake in pan, turning once until golden brown (15 min).

Serve with Wilted Spinach & slices of Red Bell Pepper.

Glazed Salmon w Zucchini

1 3/4 tbl Dijon Mustard

1 3/4 tbl Red Wine Vinegar

2 1/2 tbl Organic Honey

3/4 tsp Black Pepper (freshly ground)

1/2 tsp Himalayan Salt

Organic Olive Oil Spray

4 large Salmon Fillets

2 1/2 tbl Extra Virgin Olive Oil

1 1/4 Shallots (sliced & divided)

2 Zucchini's (3 cups) (small chunks)

3 tbs Cilantro (fresh & chopped)

Preheat the Broiler & place a rimmed baking sheet in to preheat. Mix 1/2 tsp Honey, Mustard, Vinegar, 1/4 tsp Salt, 1/4 tsp Pepper in a Glass Bowl. Microwave at HIGH for a couple of minutes. Reserve 2 tbl Honey. Remove the baking sheet from the oven & coat with the Oil Spray. Place the Salmon skin side down. Broil about 6 min. Brush the rest of the Honey mix over the Salmon. Keep warm.

Heat 1 1/2 tbl Oil in a large skillet. Add half of the Shallots, cooking for 1 1/2 min. Add 1/2 cup Zucchini cooking & stirring for 3 min. Put in a bowl. Repeat this one more time using 1 tbl Extra Virgin Olive Oil, remaining Shallots & remaining Zucchini. Add the rest of Salt & Pepper & Cilantro to Zucchini. Serve Zucchini with Salmon Fillets.

Chicken Sweet & Sour

1 lb Boneless Chicken Breast (cut 1 inch cubes)

4 1/4 tsp Cornstarch

3 Egg Whites (lg)

6 1/2 tbl Ketchup

1/4 cup Pure Water

2 tbl Brown Sugar

3 tbl Raw Apple Cider Vinegar

1 1/2 tbl Braggs Liquid Aminos

2 1/2 tbl Extra Virgin Olive Oil

1 1/2 cups Fresh Pineapple Chunks

1 Red Pepper (1 inch cubes)

2 tsp Ginger (fresh & grated)

4 Green Onions (1 inch pieces)

In a large bowl, mix Egg Whites, with 1 tbl Cornstarch stirring. Add the Chicken & mix to coat. Combine the remaining Cornstarch, Ketchup & the next 4 ingredients & keep stirring. With a large skillet, heat over medium high heat. Add 1 1/2 tbl Oil. Add Peppers, cook 2 min. Now add Pineapple, Ginger & Onions & cook for 2 min. Now put Pepper mixture to a platter. Now add 1 tbl Oil, add Chicken mix... stir-fry for 5 min. Add the Ketchup mixture & Red Pepper mixture to pan. Simmer 1 min or until thickened slightly. Sprinkle with Himalayan Salt. Enjoy!

Cod w Green Peas

3/4 cup Chicken Stock

1 1/4 tsp Fresh Mint (chopped)

1 tsp Himalayan Salt

4 (6 oz) Cod Fillets

1 1/2 tbl Extra Virgin Olive Oil

1/3 cup Lemon Juice (freshly squeezed)

2 1/2 tsp Butter

8 oz Green Peas (frozen & thawed)

1 tbl Ricotta Cheese

3 Garlic Cloves (minced)

1/2 tsp Black Pepper

1/2 cup of White Wine (dry)

2 tbl Shallots (thinly sliced)

In a food processor, add 2 tbl Chicken Stock, Ricotta, Mint, 3/8 tsp Salt & Garlic. Mix until smooth. Sprinkle Cod with remaining Salt & Pepper. Heat a skillet over medium high heat. Add 1 1/2 tbl Oil & 2 pieces of Cod. Cook 3 min on both sides. Do it again. Remove Fish from pan. Add Shallots & cook for 1 1/2 minute. Add Lemon Juice & Wine. Bring to a boil. Cook 3 min. Add Peas & boil for 2 min & then stir in Butter. On a platter, arrange Cod & Peas. Drizzle the Shallot mixture evenly over Cod & Peas. Yum!

Crabby Crab Lasagna

2 cans of Frozen Shrimp Soup (thawed)

1/2 lb Lasagne Noodles (uncooked)

2 1/2 cups Cottage Cheese (big curd)

6 oz Cream Cheese (room temp)

2 Eggs

2 tsp Basil (fresh & chopped

1 medium Onion (chopped)

2 Tomatoes (sliced)

Himalayan Salt & Freshly Ground Pepper

1 cup Cheddar Cheese (shredded)

Cook Noodles for 15 min. Combine Soup with Crabmeat & heat. Mix together the Cottage Cheese, Cream Cheese, Egg, Basil, Onion, Salt & Pepper. In a baking dish, place a layer of Noodles & cover with half of the Cheese Mixture. Top with Tomato slices. Bake 15 min in 350-degree oven.

Sprinkle the rest of Cheddar Cheese & continue baking for 30 more min. Let set 12 min after it is baked. This can also be frozen. Makes 8 servings.

Turkey & Hoisin Glazed Pork Meatloaf

4 Eggs

3/4 cup Cilantro or Fresh Parsley (minced)

5 Scallions (minced)

1/2 White Onion (finely chopped)

2 tsp toasted Sesame Oil

1 lb ground Turkey

1/3 cup Hoisin Sauce

Olive Oil cooking spray

1 1/2 cups Panko

1/3 cup of fresh Basil (minced)

7 Garlic cloves (minced)

2 1/4 tsp Himalayan Salt

1 tbl Fresh Ginger (grated)

1 lb ground Pork

2 1/2 tbl Ketchup

Preheat oven 350 degrees. In a large bowl whisk Panko, Milk, Parsley, Basil, Scallions, Garlic, Onion, Ginger, Sesame Oil, Salt & Pepper. Add Turkey & Pork. Gently combine. Shape Meat in a long loaf. Spray Loaf Pan & put in & flatten the top. Whisk Ketchup & Hoisin Sauce in a small bowl. Pour half the Sauce, coat top & sides. Bake 60 min brushing with Glaze every 20 min or so. Put the rest of Glaze over the top. Let loaf cool for 15 min. Transfer to platter.

Scallops w Oranges & Bacon

3 large Navel Oranges (divided)

1 1/2 lbs of Fresh Sea Scallops

1/2 tsp Fresh Black Pepper

2 tsp Organic Honey

5 1/2 tbl Mayonnaise

2 1/2 tsp Thyme (fresh & chopped)

5 center cut Bacon slices

1/2 tsp Himalayan Salt

2 tsp Rice Vinegar

Olive Oil Spray

2 tsp Wasabi Paste

Using a large cast iron frying pan, cook medium high until Bacon, both sides are crisp (6 min total). While Bacon is cooking, cut 1 orange in half, squeeze both halves into bowl. The other 2 Oranges just section in another bowl. Chop the cooked Bacon. Save the Bacon Grease in frying pan.

Increase heat to high. Pat Scallops dry. Sprinkle Salt & Pepper evenly over Scallops. Add Scallops to Bacon Drippings in pan. Cook 2 min on each side or until golden brown. Transfer Scallops to a platter & cover w foil to keep warm. Add Orange Juice, Vinegar, & remaining 1/4 tsp Salt to pan. Cook 2 min, scraping pan to loosen brown bits.

Drizzle Orange Juice mixture evenly over Scallops. Top evenly with Bacon, Orange Sections & fresh Thyme.

Turkey Meatballs w Spaghetti

9 oz Spaghetti

1 1/4 lb Ground Turkey

1/2 cup Parmesan Cheese

1/2 cup Italian seasoned Bread Crumbs

1/3 cup Italian Parsley (freshly chopped)

1 Egg (beaten)

3/4 cup Water

1/2 tsp Himalayan Salt

1 tbl Extra Virgin Olive Oil

3 Garlic cloves (minced)

1/2 tsp Red Pepper Flakes

1 jar Hearty Spaghetti Sauce (24 oz)

Cook Spaghetti as directed on package. Keep warm. Meanwhile, mix Turkey, Bread Crumbs, 1/4 cup Parmesan, Parsley, Egg, 1/4 cup Water & Salt. Shape mixture into Meatballs (1 1/4 in) Meatballs.

Heat Oil, Garlic, Red Peppers in a large sauté pan, medium heat. Add Sauce & remaining water once Garlic is golden. Arrange the Meatballs in Sauce, cover & cook for 10 min. Serve with hot cooked Spaghetti & Parmesan.

Bacon Broccoli Pizza

10 oz refrigerated Whole Grain Pizza Dough

5 center cut Bacon slices (chopped)

3 oz Parmigiano-Reggiano Cheese

1 cup Cherry Tomatoes (halved)

8 Shrimp (medium size & cooked)

1/2 cup Ricotta Cheese

1 tbl Extra Virgin Olive Oil

1 Garlic (large clove) (grated)

Bag of Frozen Broccoli

Place the Dough on counter at room temp… cover to prevent drying. Preheat broiler to high…. Cook Broccoli in microwave as instructed on bag. Cool slightly.

In a cast iron skillet, cook Bacon until crisp. Remove Bacon from skillet. Add the Broccoli to the drippings. Toss to coat the Broccoli with Bacon drippings. Take Broccoli out.

Combine both Cheeses with the Garlic. Mix well. Heat the skillet with medium high heat. Add Oil evenly. Remove from heat & fit the Dough which is rolled into a 10 1/2" circle. Spread the Cheese mixture evenly over Dough. Add Shrimp & Cherry Tomatoes. Cook 2 min or until the bottom is browned. Place pan in oven & broil for 2 min until Cheese is lightly browned. Top Pizza with Broccoli & Broil for 1 min.

Remove from oven & sprinkle Bacon pieces over the top.

Pork with Pineapple

2 1/2 tbl Adobo Sauce

1 Lime (fresh & squeezed)

2 cloves of Garlic (minced)

1 1/2 tbl Extra Virgin Olive Oil

1 tbl Ketchup

1/2 tsp Himalayan Salt

1/2 tsp Black Pepper

1 Pork Tenderloin (1 lb)

1/2 Pineapple (cored & cut into bite size chunks) (about 4 cups)

8 Wheat Tortillas (warmed) (6 in)

Mix Adobo Sauce with Lime Juice, Garlic, Oil, Ketchup plus Salt & Pepper. Coat the Tenderloins & marinate in fridge for an hour. Bring to room temperature before grilling. Heat the grill to medium high & spray Olive Oil on the grill.

Grill Pork turning every 5 to 6 min until light pink. (150 degrees in center) (25 min) Meanwhile, grill Pineapple (2-3 min) each side. Slice Pork & Pineapple. Serve with Tortilla's & your own toppings.

Mussels with White Wine

2 1/2 tbl Butter

1 cup Leeks (thinly sliced)

1/2 tsp Lemon Rind (grated)

2 lbs Small Mussels (cleaned)

1/4 tsp Black Pepper (freshly ground)

1 tbl Extra Virgin Olive Oil

3/4 cup White Wine (dry)

2 tbl Lemon Juice (fresh)

1/4 tsp Himalayan Salt

Heat Butter & Olive Oil in a large stockpot over medium heat. Add Leeks to pan & cook until softened. Add Wine, Lemon Rind & Lemon Juice to pan, bring to a simmer for 2 min. Add Mussels & cook until open. Remove pan from heat. Spoon Mussels into large serving bowl. Stir Salt and Pepper into broth & pour over Mussels.

Yum!!!

Sirloin Steaks w Baked Fries

3 large Potatoes

2 tsp Fresh Rosemary (chopped)

5 small lean Sirloin Steaks

3 tbl + 1 tsp Extra Virgin Olive Oil

1/2 tsp Himalayan Salt

Heat oven 425 degrees. Cut Potatoes into 1/2 inch thick wedges. Toss Potatoes with 2 tbl Oil, Rosemary & 1/4 tsp Salt.

Bake on nonstick baking sheet for 30 to 35 min until golden brown on bottoms. Turn Fries & bake until golden brown all over 10 - 15 minutes.

While Fries bake, let Steaks come to room temperature 20 to 30 min. Heat grill to medium high. Brush steaks with 1 tbl Oil +1 tsp Oil & 1/4 tsp Salt. Grill, 4 to 5 min on each side for medium rare. Yum!!!

Italian Sausage Pizza with Greens

6.5 oz Hot Italian Turkey Sausage (about 2 links)

1 lb Whole Wheat Pizza Dough (fresh & unfrozen)

1 Collard Greens (small bunch)

3/4 cup Ricotta Cheese

2 cloves of Garlic (thinly sliced)

1 1/4 tbl Extra Virgin Olive Oil

Baby Arugula

1/2 tsp Himalayan Salt

1/2 tsp Red Pepper Flakes

Heat oven 400 degrees. Bring a large pot of water to a boil. Cook the Sausage in a skillet over medium heat. Using a wooden spoon break up the sausage until browned (6 min). Use paper towels to drain on.

Cook Collard Greens in the boiling water stirring for 1 min. Drain & rinse under cold water & squeeze dry. Coarsely chop.

Stretch dough in shape of a rectangular on parchment paper lined baking sheet. Arrange Collard Greens & Sausage on top of dough. Dollop with Ricotta, Garlic Sprinkles & drizzle with Oil. Bake about 25 min & top with Arugula, Salt & Red Pepper Flakes.

Shrimp Lemon Herb Risotto

2 1/2 cups Chicken Stock

1 cup Water

1/2 cup Yellow Onion (finely chopped)

1/4 cup Fennel Bulb (finely chopped

1 tbl Extra Virgin Olive Oil

1 tbl Thyme (fresh) (finely chopped)

3 Garlic cloves (minced)

3/4 cup uncooked Arborio Rice

3/4 cup White Wine (dry)

3/4 cup fresh French Green Beans

1/2 tsp Himalayan Salt

9 oz Shrimp (peeled & deveined)

1 tbl Cream Cheese

1 1/2 tbl Lemon Juice (freshly squeezed)

2 tsp Lemon Rind (grated)

1/2 tsp of White Pepper

1 tbl Fennel Fronds (chopped)

Combine Stock & Water in a large glass bowl. Microwave on high for 2 min or until warm. Heat oil in a large saucepan adding Garlic, Onion, Fennel, and Thyme… Sauté for 4 minutes. Add Wine & cook another minute. Add Rice & cook for 1 min, stirring constantly. Add 1 cup Stock & cook for about 4 minutes until liquid has almost evaporated. Add the rest of Stock (saving 1/2 cup for later) slowly with 1/2 cup at a time until absorbed while stirring constantly for about 14 min. Stir in 1/4 cup Stock, Beans & Salt. Cook until liquid is absorbed. Stir in remaining 1/4 cup Stock & rest of ingredients. Serve immediately.

Before Desserts

OK.… So you are all geared up to stuff yourself with desserts. Yes, desserts can be fattening so we will try to help you from getting a fat gut & a large lard ass. All of our dessert recipes have been worked over to lower the calorie count. We hope that you will enjoy trying all of them but don't eat all of them in one sitting.

Desserts

Angel Food Roll w Berries

Rich Chocolate Decadent Mousse

Blueberry Crisp

Rummy Rum Balls

Aunt Ruby's Coconut Custard Pie

Pear Clafoutis

Apple Walnut Crisp

Bourbon Cherry Crisp

Apple Raspberry Coconut Crisp

Cranberry Poached Pears

The Best Carrot Cake Ever

Almond Apricot Cake

Tangy Lemon Cheesecake Bars

Luscious Lemon Pie

Scrumptious Brownies

Angel Food Roll w Berries

Angel Food Cake Mix
1/4 cup Powdered Sugar plus
1/4 cup Powdered Sugar
8 oz Light Cream Cheese (room temp)
1 tsp Vanilla

1 1/3 cups of Heavy Cream
1 1/3 cups Strawberries (freshly sliced)
1 1/3 cups Blueberries fresh)
1 1/3 cup Raspberries (fresh)

Preheat oven 350 degrees. Using parchment paper, line the bottom of a pan size approx. 10 X 15 inches.

Mix up the Angel Food Cake. Pour cake batter in pan & bake for about 17 min until the top is golden & springs back when lightly touched. Using a knife loosen the edges. Flip the cake on top of a towel with the Powdered Sugar evenly spread. Remove parchment paper. Roll the cake in the towel & let cool for 2 hours.

Mix the Cream Cheese with a mixer in a large bowl. Then add the other Powdered Sugar & beat on high until fluffy & peaks form. Unroll the cooled cake & spread with half of the filling. Put 1/2 of the Berries on top of icing & roll back up.

Spread the top & sides with the icing & rest of Berries. Yum!

Rich Decadent Chocolate Mousse

1/4 cup Coconut Milk

8 Dates that are pitted (finely chopped)

1 tbl unsweetened Cocoa

3 oz bittersweet Chocolate (chopped)

3/4 tsp Vanilla

8 oz silken Tofu

1/4 cup Sour Cream

3 lg Egg Whites

Mix Coconut Milk with Dates in a small saucepan. Bring to a boil. Simmer for 2 min. With a slotted spoon, remove Dates & set aside. Add Cocoa & simmer for 1 min. Stir in bittersweet Chocolate & stir until the Chocolate has melted. Stir in Vanilla.

Place Tofu, Sour Cream & Dates in a blender & blend until smooth. Add Chocolate mixture to Tofu. Blend some more. Pour in a bowl. In another bowl, beat Egg Whites until stiff peaks form. Fold Egg Whites into Chocolate mixture. Put in ramekins & refrigerate for 8 hours.

Blueberry Crisp

Filling:

6 1/2 cups Blueberries (fresh or frozen)

1/3 cup Brown Sugar

1 tsp Lemon Zest (grated)

Topping:

2/3 cup Whole Wheat Flour

1/2 cup Rolled Oats

1/2 cup Brown Sugar (packed)

6 tbl Olive Oil

1 tsp Cinnamon

1/4 tsp Himalayan Salt

Preheat oven 375 degrees. Combine topping ingredients in a bowl. Mix until combined & crumbly. Mix Blueberries w Sugar & Lemon Zest. Pour into a 9-inch square pan. Cover with topping. Bake until the Berry Juices are bubbly & the topping is browned, about 65 min. Remove to wire rack. Serve warm.

Rummy Rum Balls

3 cups crushed Vanilla Wafers

1 cup Powdered Sugar

1 1/4 cups Walnuts (chopped)

2 tbl Cocoa Powder

2/3 cup Rum

2 1/2 tbl light Corn Syrup

Place Wafers in zip lock bag & with rolling pin until finely crushed. Mix with Walnuts, Powdered Sugar & Cocoa. Add Corn Syrup, Rum & mix well.

Roll into balls the size of walnuts. Roll in extra Powdered Sugar. Store in metal container.

Aunt Ruby's Coconut Custard Pie

Crust:

1 3/4 cups w 2 tbl Wheat Flour

3/4 tsp Himalayan Salt

5 tbl Vegetable Shortening

5 tbl Unsalted Butter (cut in small cubes)

1/4 cup Ice Water

Filling:

1 cup Organic Sugar

4 tbl Unsalted Butter (melted)

6 Eggs (large)

1 cup Buttermilk

Himalayan Salt

2 cups Sweetened Coconut (shredded) Vanilla Ice Cream

Crust:

Whisk Flour w Salt in medium bowl using pastry blender, cut in Shortening & Butter to small pieces. Stir in Water until dough consistency. Refrigerate until well chilled. After cooling, roll out dough to a 12 inch round. Place in 9-inch glass pie plate. Trim off dough that hangs over & crimp the edges. Chill for 20 min.

Preheat oven 375. Put in oven for 20 min covering pie rims with foil. Take out & let cool. Lower oven temperature to 350 degrees.

Filling:

Whisk Sugar w Butter, then Eggs. Add Buttermilk, Vanilla with Salt & add Coconut.

Pour filling into piecrust & bake for 40 - 45 min until custard is golden brown. Remove foil, slice pie wedges & serve w Ice Cream.

Pear Clafoutis

2 large ripe Pears (peeled, cored & sliced)

3 tbl Pear Brandy

1/2 cup Organic Sugar

3 Eggs

1 1/4 tsp Vanilla Extract

1/4 tsp Himalayan Salt

1/2 cup Whole Wheat Flour

1 tsp Powdered Sugar

Preheat oven 350 degrees. Butter a medium cast iron skillet. Combine Pears, Pear Brandy & Sugar. Let stand for 30 min. Pour the liquid from the Pears into a blender. Add the remaining ingredients. Blend at high speed for a minute. Arrange Pears on bottom of skillet. Pour the batter over the Pears. Put in oven & bake for 50 min. Sprinkle Powdered Sugar over the top. Serve warm or chilled.

Apple Walnut Crisp

1/2 cup Organic Sugar

1/2 tsp Cinnamon

1/2 tsp Nutmeg

1/2 cup Walnuts (chopped)

4 cups Apples (thinly sliced)

1 cup Whole Wheat Flour (sifted)

1 cup Organic Sugar

1 tsp Baking Powder

1/4 tsp Himalayan Salt

1 Egg (beaten)

1/2 cup 2% Milk

1/3 cup Butter (melted)

Mix 1/2-cup Organic Sugar, Cinnamon, Nutmeg & 1/3 of Walnuts. Place Apples in bottom of greased baking dish. Combine Egg, Milk, & Butter. Now add the dry ingredients to the liquid & mix until smooth. Pour over the Apples. Sprinkle the remaining 1/4 cup Walnuts. Bake in 325 degrees for 50 min. Serve with Whip Cream.

Bourbon Cherry Crisp

Bourbon:

1/2 cup Dried Cherries

3/4 cup Bourbon

Crumble:

1 3/4 cups Whole Wheat Flour

1/2 cup Organic Sugar

2/3 cup Dark Brown Sugar

1/2 tsp Salt

1/4 tsp Ground Cinnamon

1/4 tsp Nutmeg (grated)

12 tbl Butter (cold & cubed)

Assemble:

5 cups pitted Cherries

3 tbl Organic Sugar

3 tbl Orange Juice

1/4 tsp Salt

Vanilla Ice Cream

Make Bourbon Cherries. Let sit for 4 hours. Make crumble topping: Mix all the dry ingredients together & add Butter using fingers to mix until very small pieces. Chill for 30 min. Preheat oven to 350 degrees. Assemble & bake crumbles: in a large bowl, combine fresh Cherries; Bourbon soaked Cherries, Sugar, Orange Juice & Salt. Pour into a 9-inch square baking pan. Top with crumble topping. Bake until golden brown & bubbling Cherries. 35 min. Serve warm with Vanilla Ice Cream.

Apple Raspberry Coconut Crisp

1 cup plus 1 tbl Whole Wheat Flour

1/2 cup plus 1tbl packed Brown Sugar

1/2 tsp Salt

1/4 tsp Cinnamon

1/4 tsp Baking Powder

1/4 cup sliced Almonds

1/2 cup Coconut Oil

8 Granny Apples (small) (peeled, cored & sliced)

2 six oz. containers of Raspberries

Preheat oven to 375 degrees. Mix 1 cup Flour with packed Brown Sugar, Cinnamon, Salt & Baking Soda. Using your fingers, work the Coconut Oil into the Flour mixture until coarse crumbs form. Add Almonds & mix to combine. Chill. Toss Apples, Raspberries, 1 tbl Flour, & 1 tbl Brown Sugar in a large bowl. Put in a 9 X 13 in baking pan. Sprinkle the topping over the fruit & bake until brown & bubbling. 30 min. Serve with Vanilla Ice Cream.

Cranberry Poached Pears

8 Pears (small, peels w stems in tact)

5 tbl Organic Honey

3 tbl Organic Sugar

1 Orange Zest (4 - 5 inches)

1 Lemon Zest (4 - 5 inches)

1 tsp Lemon Juice (fresh)

1 Cinnamon Stick (3 min)

1 Vanilla Bean (split lengthwise in half)

1 Fruit Tea Bag (passion fruit)

2 1/4 cups Fresh Cranberries

Place Pears in Saucepan large enough to hold them snugly. Add enough Water to barely cover them. Add Honey, Sugar, Lemon & Orange Zest with Lemon Juice & Cinnamon Stick. Using a paring knife, scrape Vanilla seeds out of pod & add to pan. Bring to a boil over med heat until the sugar is dissolved. Reduce heat & simmer until Pears are tender with a tip of knife. 10 minutes. Add Cranberries & simmer until they burst, about 3 min. Remove & discard the Tea Bag. Take the Pears to a large bowl & pour Cranberries & Syrup over them. Cover & refrigerate for three days. Remove & discard the Citrus Zest, Cinnamon Stick & Vanilla Bean. Arrange Pears on a platter…. spoon the Cranberries & as much of the poaching liquid as desired. Serve.

The Best Carrot Cake Ever

6 cups Carrots (grated)

1 cup Brown Sugar

1 cup Raisins

4 Eggs

1 1/2 cups organic Sugar

1 cup Vegetable Oil

1 cup crushed Pineapple (drained)

3 cups Whole Wheat Flour

1 1/2 tsp Baking Soda

1 tsp Himalayan Salt

4 tsp Ground Cinnamon

1 cup Walnuts (chopped)

In medium bowl, combine grated Carrots & Brown Sugar. Preheat oven 350 degrees. Grease & Flour 2 (10 inch) cake pans.

In large bowl, beat Eggs & gradually add in white Sugar, Oil & Vanilla. Stir in Pineapple. Combine Flour, Soda, Salt & Cinnamon. Stir in wet mixture. Finally stir in Carrot mixture & Walnuts. Pour into cake pans. Bake 45 to 50 min until cake tests done with a toothpick. Cool 10 min & remove cake. Add Cream Cheese frosting after cooled.

Almond Apricot Cake

3 1/2 cups Almonds (sliced)

3 tbl Matzo Cake Meal

8 large Eggs (room temp)(seperate)

1 cup plus 4 tbl Organic Sugar

1 tsp Orange Zest (grated)

1 tsp Lemon Zest plus 2 tbl Lemon Juice

1 tsp Almond Extract

1/4 tsp Himalayan Salt

1 lb Apricots (dried) (finely chopped) Whipped Cream

Preheat oven 350 degrees. Coat two round pans using cooking spray & line the bottoms w parchment paper. Spray the paper too. In food processor put 2 1/2 cups Almonds & Cake Meal until finely ground. On a baking sheet, toast the remaining Almonds & put to the side. Using an electric mixer beat the Egg Yolks & gradually beat in 1 cup Sugar. Increase the speed & beat until the batter leaves a trail. 4-5 min. Beat in the Orange & Lemon Zests & Almond Extract. Fold in the nut mixture. Using another bowl, beat the Egg Whites with Salt until foamy. Increase speed until stiff peaks form. Stir in half the Egg Whites into the Yolk mixture. Then fold in the rest of the Egg Whites until no streaks remain. Divide the batter between the pans. Bake until a toothpick inserted comes out dry. 23 to 25 minutes. Cool. Meanwhile place the Apricots in a small saucepan & add the fresh Lemon Juice & remaining 2 tbl Sugar. Cover with water (2 cups) & bring to boil. Reduce heat & simmer for about 20 min. Transfer to food processor & puree. Spread 3/4 cup of Apricots on one inverted cake layer. Now place the other cake on top & spread the remaining Apricot mixture on the top & sides. Press sliced Almonds on top & sides. Serve with Whipped Cream.

Tangy Lemon Cheesecake Bars

1 cup Whole Wheat Flour

1/2 cup Almonds (toasted & sliced)

3 tbl Powdered Sugar

1 tbl Extra Virgin Olive Oil

1/4 tsp Himalayan Salt

1/4 cup Cold Butter (cut into tiny cubes) Olive Oil Cooking Spray

Filling:

3/4 cup Greek Yogurt

1/2 cup Organic Sugar

1 1/2 tbl Lemon Rind (grated)

1/3 cup + 1 tbl Lemon Juice (fresh)

1 1/4 tsp Vanilla Extract

1/4 tsp Himalayan Salt

1 Cream Cheese (8 oz pkg)

2 large Eggs

Preheat over 350 degrees. Put Flour, Almonds, Powdered Sugar, Oil & Salt in a food processor until Almonds are finely ground. Add Butter, pulse until medium sized. Pour in 11" X 7" baking dish. Spray Olive Oil in dish. Now pat the mixture lightly in the pan. Bake 22 minutes or until browned lightly. Remove from oven & cool. Reduce oven temperature to 325 degrees.

Filling: Put Yogurt & next 6 ingredients in a clean food processor. Pulse until smooth. Add Eggs & pulse. Pour the mixture into the crust. Bake for about 30 min. Remove from oven & cool completely. Refrigerate for 24 hours. Serve.

Luscious Lemon Pie

1 cup Organic Sugar

1/4 cup Cornstarch

1/4 tsp Himalayan Salt

2 cups Water

3 Egg Yolks (beaten)

1 tbl Butter

1/4 cup Lemon Juice (fresh)

1 tsp Lemon Zest (grated) Pastry Shell

Meringue:

3 Egg Whites

1/4 tsp Himalayan Salt

1/2 cup Organic Sugar

Garnish:

Slice of Lemon

In medium saucepan, mix Sugar, Cornstarch, Whole Wheat Flour & Salt. Gradually stir in Water. Cook & stir over medium heat & gradually stir in 1 cup of hot mixture into Egg Yolks. Bring to boil & stir for 2 min. Remove from heat. Stir in Butter, Lemon Juice & Zest until smooth. Pour into Pastry Shell. Chill for 8 hours. In another bowl, beat Egg Whites. Gradually beat in Sugar until soft peaks form. Spread on top of Lemon Pie. Garnish with a slice of Lemon. Yum!!!

Scrumptious Brownies

1 cup Organic Sugar

3 tbl Irish Butter (melted)

3 tbl Greek Vanilla Yogurt

1 Egg (slightly beaten)

3/4 cup Whole Wheat Flour

1/3 cup Cocoa

1/4 tsp Himalayan Salt

Fresh Strawberries cut in half

Preheat oven 350 degrees. In a small bowl, combine the Sugar, Butter, Yogurt & Vanilla. Then stir in Egg until blended. Mix in the Flour, Cocoa & Salt. Stir in Sugar mixture. Put in an 8 inch Baking Dish coated in Olive Oil Spray. Bake for 22 minutes. Take out & place on cooling rack. Decorate Brownie square with fresh Strawberries. Yum!!!

Super Foods = Super Health

Broccoli: Loaded with Vit C, Carotinoids, Vit K & Folate.

Leafy Greens: Loade with Vit A, C & K, Folate, Potassium, Magnesium, Calcium, Iron & Fiber.

Betternut Squash: Contains lots of Vit A & C & Fiber.

Sweet Potatoes: Loaded with Carotenoids & are a good source of Potassium & Fiber.

Garbanzo Beans: Rich in Protein, Fiber, Copper, Folate, Iron, Magnesium, Potassium & Zinc.

Mangoes: One cup supplies 100% of a days Vit C, 1/3 of a days Vit A.

Watermelon: 2 cups has 1/3 of a days Vit A & C, Potassium, Lycopene.

Plain Greek Yogurt: Has twice the Protein of ordinary Yogurt. Wild Salmon: Rich in Omega 3 fats. Helps reduce the risk of heart attacks & strokes.

Oatmeal: Contains Fiber. Helps lower cholesterol.

Kitchen Tips

When grilling steaks, sometimes the edges can curl & the meat no longer sits flat in the pan or on the grill. To help prevent that, cut a slit in the fat along the edge of the meat every inch or so before cooking.

Keep 2 bay leaves in the canister of flour to help deter flour weevils from proliferating. You can toss the leaves loose in the flour, make a rough pouch of one layer of cheesecloth to keep the leaves separated from the flour or you can tape the bay leaves to the inside of the lid.

Separate Eggs with a funnel....If you don't have an egg separator & need a yolk or egg white for a recipe, you use a small funnel. Gently crack the egg & break into funnel…. No funnel? Clip a corner off a plastic bag & use that as a funnel.

Clean as you go! Not only is cleaning up after you've eaten, the last thing you will be wanting to do. The food has probably congealed so you'll have to spend even longer cleaning it all away. The trick is to clear as you go…. have a trash can close by so you put wrappers, peelings, etc. straight into it, load the dishwasher as you go, rinse cans for recycling as you use them, etc. This time you save, adds up.

Kitchen Tips

Bacon can be quite a mess item to prepare. Try lightly dusting the bacon with flour before frying. Helps prevent splatters & meat shrinkage.

Keep cookies moist & chewy by throwing a few slices of apple in your cookie jar to keep cookies soft. Don't do this if you like crispy or crunchy cookies.

Rinse measuring cup in hot water before using syrup, oil, etc. It will pour out clean & not stick to the cup.

Stay organized. Keep the most used items in an easy reach. The least used items farther away. Place your plates, cups, cutlery as close to the dishwasher/sink as possible. Save time & put away after being cleaned.

Take the extra oven rack when baking & you can it for the cooling rack. Works for cookies, cakes or hors d' oeuvres, whatever you like. If you are baking smaller items that might fall through, cover the rack with foil.

Works like a charm.

Coffee Tip

People who drink three to five cups of coffee per day, have a 15% lower chance of diabetes & heart disease than those who don't sip java. This was a quote from a recent Harvard study. Black Coffee is the best.

Good-bye Friends,

It has been very enjoyable traveling through this Cook Book with you. You have stuck with using recipes that include healthy & tasty ingredients.

For the last recipe in the book, we'll give you permission to let all hell pop loose & you can have the pleasure of making something sweet, gooey & unhealthy. We're sharing our Almond Roca Candy recipe.

I (Myrtle) make it once a year & give it away as Christmas Gifts.

Almond Roca Candy

2 cups Organic Sugar

3 cubes of Butter

1 1/2 cups Chocolate Chips

1 1/2 cups Almonds (chopped)

1/2 Walnuts (chopped)

Stir over low heat & when it comes to a boil, add 1 1/2 cups whole Almonds. Turn to medium heat or a little above med. Stir continuously until your candy thermometer reads 310. Remove from heat & pour onto lightly greased 8 1/2 inch by 11 inch cookie sheet. Let stand a few minutes & lay 1 1/2 cup Chocolate Chips evenly over all. Take another cookie sheet….. Cover for 5 to 10 minutes…. after that spread melted Chocolate over all. Sprinkle chopped Walnuts over all. Cool overnight before breaking into small pieces.

CPSIA information can be obtained
at www.ICGtesting.com
Printed in the USA
BVHW090842240619
551798BV00012B/375